MONSTERS OF THE DEEP

Contents

Written by Alison Hawes

Sharks

This shark is a hunter and a killer.
Its sharp teeth can snap animals
in half!

This big shark is harmless.
It is a filter feeder.
It filters krill through its gills.

This monster shark is the biggest shark of all.

It is bigger than a bus!

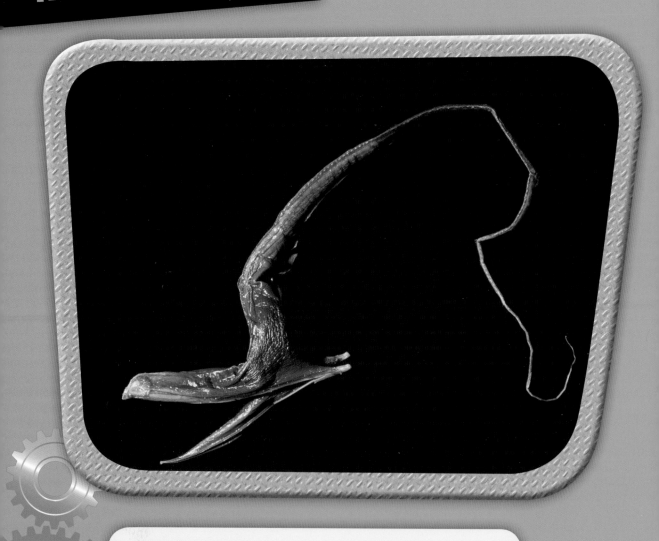

This gulper eel can feed on fish bigger than itself!

Monster Squid

This is a monster of the deep. Squid have long arms with suckers on them.

It is longer than three buses!

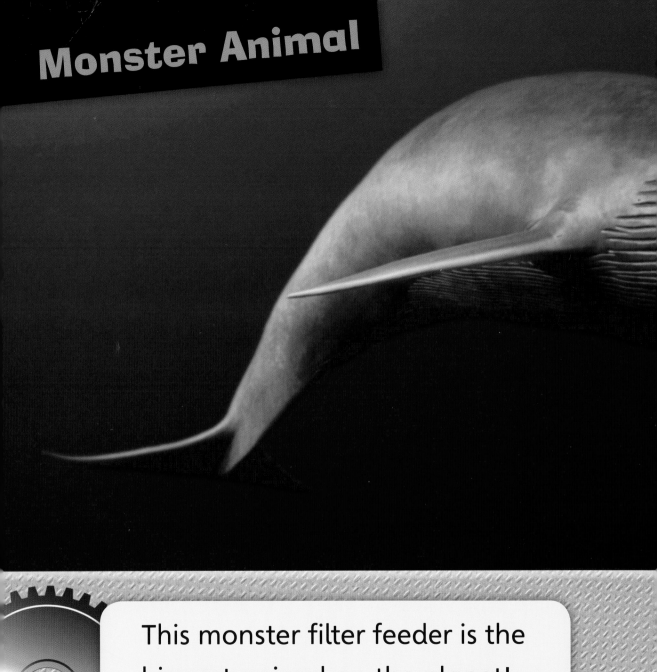

This monster filter feeder is the biggest animal on the planet!

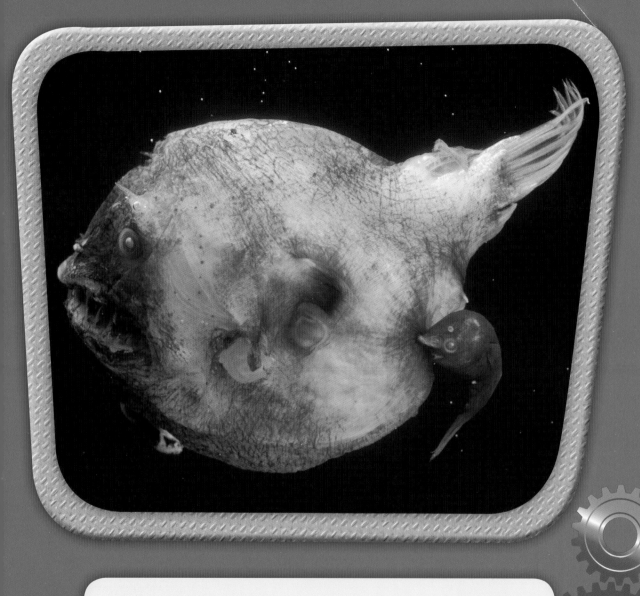

But the mum angler fish is much bigger than the dad!